CONTENTS

For new surfing fans, surfing words are explained on page 30.

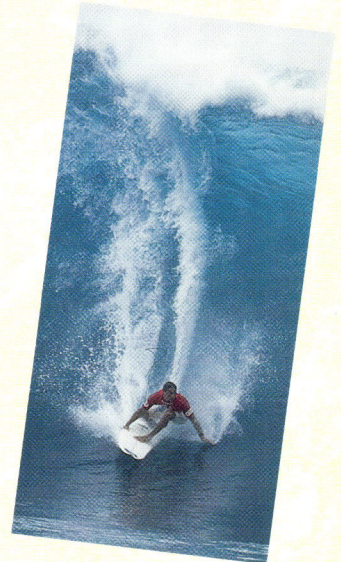

I AM A SURF FREAK

Dan Johnson Fact File:
Age: sixteen
Years riding: two
Favourite foods: spaghetti bolognese, barbecued sausages on the beach
Hobbies: surfing, computer games, skateboarding, playing guitar

This is me!

I am Dan Johnson, and this is my story. I'm a surf addict. I'm addicted to waves, they draw me back again and again. Surfing has led me to sit shivering in the sea when it's at its coldest. I've missed Christmas dinner with my family, fallen out with my girlfriend, and spent all my spare money. Normal people look at me strangely: my clothes are different, my hair's different – I'm different, to everyone except other surfers.

This book is a collection of pages from my diary and scrapbook. It tells the story of my surf addiction.

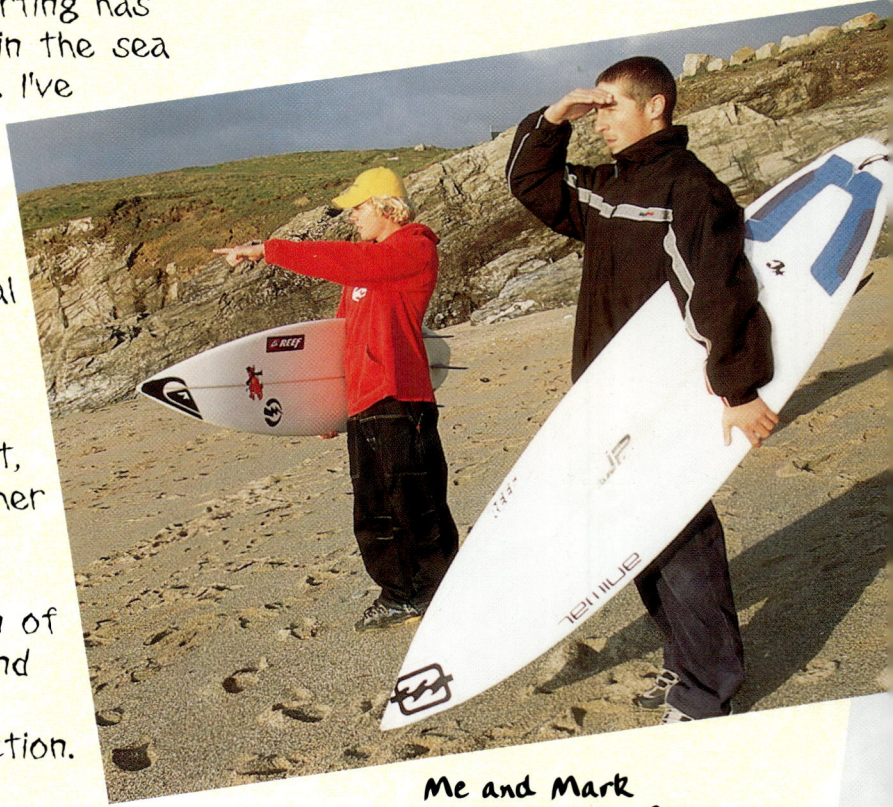

Me and Mark checking out the surf.

4

Busting the fins out on a turn!

MAY

5	12	19	26
6	13	20	27
7	14	21	28
1	8	15	22	29
2	9	16	23	30
3	10	17	24	31
4	11	18	25

Dad took these of the first-ever wave I managed to stand up on (for about three seconds!).

SATURDAY 10 MAY
THE EARLY DAYS

My first proper weekend living here on the coast. Some of the guys I met at my new school persuaded me to come out surfing with them today. I thought I'd be good at it because I'm OK at skateboarding. But surfing's very different, and seemed much harder!

Most people were really friendly, but one surfer kept bellowing 'My wave!' at me. Someone told my Dad, who was on the beach taking photos (embarrassing!) that I'd 'dropped in' on him. Had no idea what this meant. Need to check out the rules (and language) of surfing!

Had to fall off a lot before I managed to stand up!

6

Safe-Surfing Guidelines

Ignore these at your peril!

...1...
Only one surfer rides each wave.

...2...
The surfer closest to the (peak) gets the wave.

...3...
On a wave with more than one peak, the surfer first to their feet gets the wave.

...4...
Surfers riding waves have to avoid people paddling out.

...5...
Do not let go of your board in the whitewater.

Huh?

PEAK
WHERE A WAVE FIRST 'BREAKS' (FOLDS ON ITSELF AND BECOMES FOAMY).

FACE
OPEN PART OF A WAVE, WHICH HASN'T BROKEN YET.

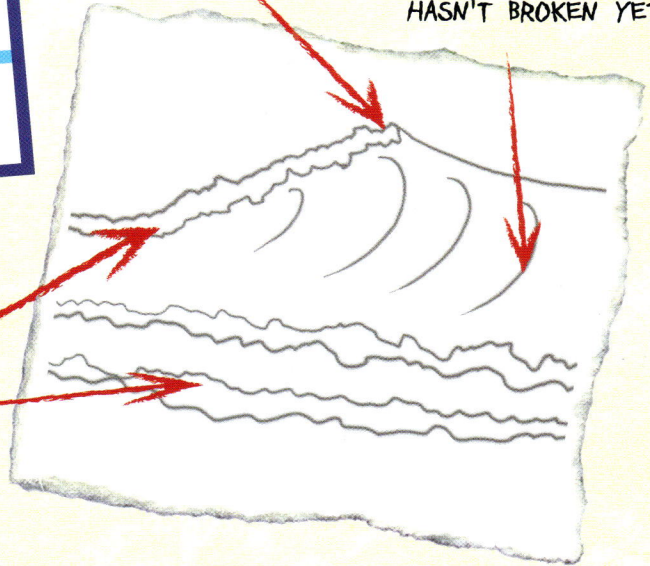

WHITEWATER
THE WHITE, FOAMY PART OF A WAVE WHICH IS THERE AFTER IT'S 'BROKEN'.

Bodyboarding looked like a good way to get used to the surf.

7

JUNE

2	9	16	23	30
3	10	17	24	
4	11	18	25	
5	12	19	26	
6	13	20	27	
7	14	21	28	
1 8	15	22	29	

Really good waves for learning today! Not too big, and really clean (no bumps on them!). We took turns taking photos of each other from the beach. Darren got some really good ones of me! I waited to catch the waves just at the place where they were breaking.

SATURDAY 28 JUNE
TAKING OFF

Have definitely had a good day today! At last I managed to get to my feet more times than not. I will soon be a master of the 'take-off'. This is the hardest thing to learn, apparently — it's definitely taken me long enough. The trick is timing the moment you get to your feet. Too soon and the board doesn't 'catch' the wave, so you get left behind. Too late and the wave throws you down in front of itself (called 'getting pitched') and you get pummelled ('trashed').

PADDLING FOR A LITTLE ONE THAT'S ABOUT TO BREAK. KEEP YOUR WEIGHT IN THE MIDDLE: TOO FAR FORWARD AND THE NOSE SINKS, TOO FAR BACK AND YOU'RE PUSHING WATER IN FRONT OF YOU.

PUSHING DOWN ON THE DECK, READY TO WHIP MY FEET THROUGH. SAW SOME PEOPLE KNEELING THEN STANDING UP, TO HELP THEM BALANCE. EITHER WAY, GET UP JUST AS THE BOARD CATCHES THE WAVE, AND STAND WITH YOUR FEET ACROSS THE CENTRE OF THE BOARD.

8

STANDING UP ON A BIG ONE. DON'T REMEMBER THEM BEING THIS BIG!

TURNING THE BOARD ALONG THE WAVE BY LEANING IT IN THE DIRECTION I WANTED TO GO WITH MORE WEIGHT ON MY BACK FOOT. I LOOK LIKE A GOOD SURFER! YAY!

Had to buy my own wetsuit kit, as my friend Mark's old wetsuit was too small and too stinky. I'm sure he used to wee in it—smells like it, anyway!

SUMMER SUIT — made of neoprene that's 2 mm or 3 mm thick.

RASH VEST — to stop wetsuit rubbing your skin raw.

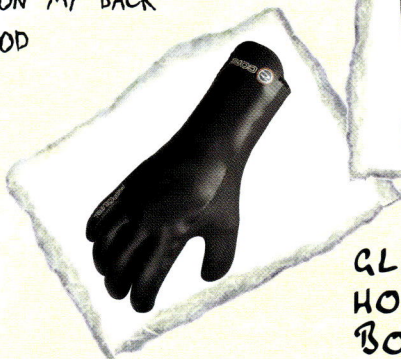

GLOVES, HOOD AND BOOTS — for when it's cold!

9

JULY

	7	14	21	28
1	8	15	22	29
2	9	16	23	30
3	10	17	24	31
4	11	18	25	
5	12	19	26	
6	13	20	27	

My new stick from the deck (the top). It won't ever be this shiny and new again! Wider nose and tail so that it floats well in smaller waves.

THURSDAY 31 JULY
BOARD

My birthday; also just finished school for summer so can go surfing every day! Got the best present I could imagine, which was a surfboard. I went down to one of the local shops with an idea of what I wanted, and the salesman helped me narrow the choice down to one board (or 'stick'). He even threw in a leash and some wax for free!

Waxing up for the first time! The wax stops my feet slipping: just rub it on and you're ready to go!

View from the side. Not too much rocker (curve), so it should catch waves well.

NEW STICK FACT FILE:

Dimensions:
6' 6" long, 19.5" wide, 2.5" thick

Outline shape:
wider nose and tail

Tail shape and fins:
squash tail, three fins

FUNBOARD

USUALLY ABOUT 7' 2" LONG WITH THREE FINS, THESE CATCH WAVES WELL BUT AREN'T MANOEUVRABLE ENOUGH FOR ME!

LONGBOARD

9'–9' 6" LONG WITH EITHER ONE OR THREE FINS, GOOD FOR CATCHING LOTS OF WAVES BUT VERY HEAVY AND SLOW-TURNING.

GUN

7'–9' LONG, WITH ONE OR THREE FINS. FOR BIG WAVES AND EXPERTS ONLY!

NOTE: Surfboard measurements are always in feet and inches, not metric.

SARAH

I recently discovered I've got an American cousin who's into surfing too. She mailed me some photos. It looks a lot warmer there than it is here!

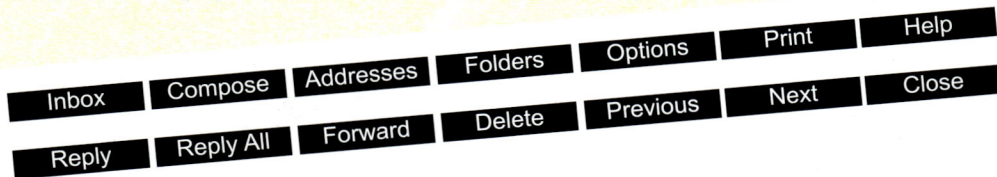

Inbox   Compose   Addresses   Folders   Options   Print   Help

Reply   Reply All   Forward   Delete   Previous   Next   Close

From: sarah
Date: Monday, August 18
To: dan
Subject: bottom!

>Hey, Dan!

>It was great to meet you at the wedding: I had no idea there would be any other surfers there, let alone one who's my cousin! As promised I'm sending you some photos of myself out at my local break. Also attached are some photos of other female surfers – see, girls do surf, and good! Check out Rochelle Ballard's shack time if you still don't believe me! (She's a Hawaiian pro surfer, in case you haven't heard.)

>I'm still struggling with my bottom turn, when I've just caught the wave and stood up. I know this is the basic manoeuvre for performance surfing, the one that sets up all other moves, so I need to get it right. The one in the photo isn't too bad, but when you look at the photo of Joel Parkinson you can see there could be a lot more power in my version! Are you still finding this tricky too? Any hints gratefully received.

>Email me soon and let me know.

>Sarah

>PS Has the water warmed up for you yet? Note that we're not even wearing wetsuits here in San Diego right now!

12

Sitting in the line-up, waiting for waves.

Lisa Andersen floater.

Backhand bottom turn.

Joel Parkinson, high-speed bottom turn!

Trudy Todd cutback.

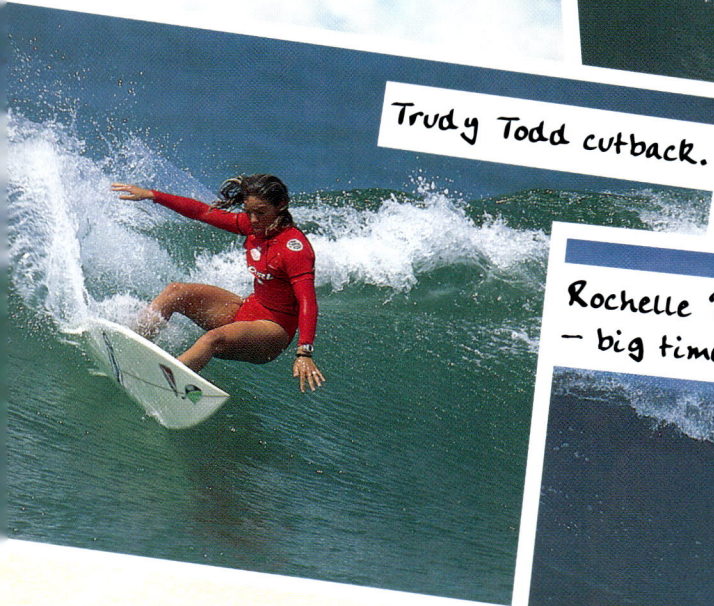

Rochelle Ballard in the tube — big time shack time!

AUGUST

4	11	18	25
5	12	19	26
6	13	20	27
7	14	21	28
1	8	15	22	29
2	9	16	23	30
3	10	17	24	31

FRIDAY 22 AUGUST
BOTTOM TURN

After my cousin Sarah's email from California, I decided to go to the beach with Mark and Darren to take some bottom-turn photos. We thought it might help her, but it turned out to be a little harder than expected! I managed to get one photo of myself, and that was it.

Did find some good photos in a magazine, so am going to send a copy to Sarah for her to have a look at.

BOTTOM-TURN TECHNIQUE (FRONT-SIDE)

1 Keep your knees bent as you go down the face of the wave.

2 When you reach the bottom part of the wave, push down with your toes and lean your weight into the turn.

3 As the board comes round straighten your legs to get more power into the turn.

4 When the board starts to head back up the wave, ease off the turn by putting your weight more over the centre line of the board, so that you're travelling along the wave.

At last, a decent bottom turn by me!

KALANI ROBB, BACK-HAND BOTTOM TURN.

ONE OF THE LOCAL
PRO SURFERS CHARGING
IN BIG SURF.

ROB MACHADO AT
PIPELINE, HAWAII:
BOTTOM TURN TO
TUBE RIDE.

15

AUGUST

```
        4   11   18   25
        5   12   19   26
        6   13   20   27
        7   14   21   28
   1    8   15   22   29
   2    9   16   23   30
   3   10   17   24   31
```

CUTBACK SEQUENCE — I KEPT MY KNEES BENT AND MY BODY LOW TO PUSH THROUGH A REALLY TIGHT TURN.

SUNDAY 24 AUGUST
SUMMER SWELL

Good swell at the moment. I'm surfing for six hours a day, to make the most of the waves while they're here! We spent all day Friday and yesterday working on basic techniques: first bottom turns, then cutbacks (when you turn to change direction on the wave), floaters (riding the foamy section of wave after it has broken) and top turns (a move to pick up speed and power). Mark's dad has a good digital camera: he took a load of photos, and we just printed them off the computer.

MARK RIPS! MASSIVE HIGH—SPEED TOP TURN ON A DECENT—SIZED WAVE.

THIS WAS MY FIRST PROPER FLOATER. A FLOATER LIKE THIS WILL GET ME PAST BIG SECTIONS OF WHITEWATER AND BACK ON TO THE FACE OF THE WAVE.

SEPTEMBER

1	8	15	22	29
2	9	16	23	30
3	10	17	24	
4	11	18	25	
5	12	19	26	
6	13	20	27	
7	14	21	28	

Our campsite in the dunes, with the surf break in the background!

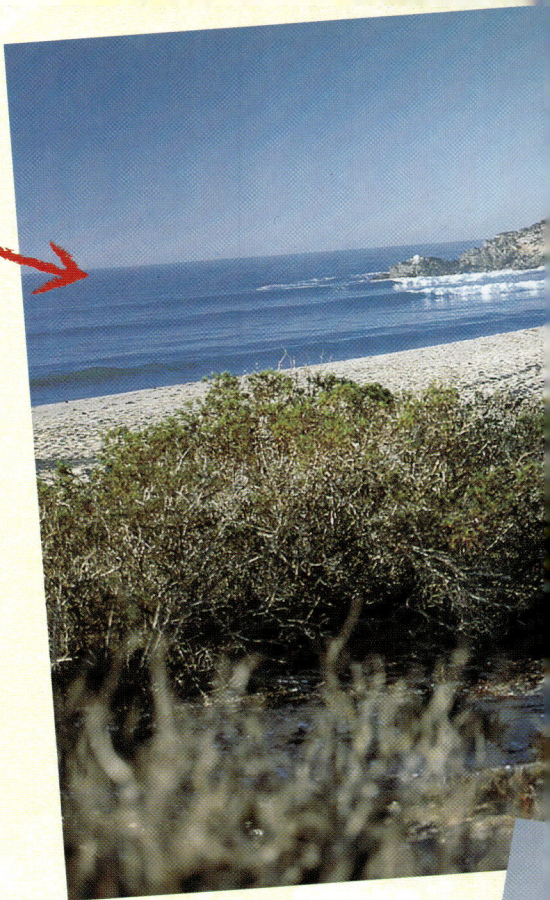

SUNDAY 21 SEPTEMBER
SURF TRIP

Soooo tired! We just got back – at about 1 a.m. – from a big surf trip. We'd had it planned for a long time: got an Internet guide for the area we wanted to surf, had the tents and sleeping bags ready. All we were waiting for was the swell, and the Internet sites were predicting good surf this weekend. They weren't wrong!

We had a fantastic trip, but I was really glad we'd made the checklist before we left. If we'd forgotten to take water, for example, it would have been a big problem.

... and even later that night.

STUFF WE NEED:

• Tents, sleeping bags, sleep mats. Pillows for softies! Make sure all poles and pegs are in with tents.

• Wash kit.

• First aid kit, plus board repair kit (first aid for boards!).

• Camp stove and fuel, knives, forks and spoons.

• Food: loads of pasta and cheese— it's all we can cook! Breakfast things, cereal. Need to eat loads of carbohydrates (pasta) to keep our energy up, and slow-burn fats (cheese) for warmth.

• Big water containers, as there's none on the beach we're camping at.

• Ear plugs to block out the terrible snoring!

This was two bays further down the coast, along a very dusty track.

SEPTEMBER

1	8	15	22	29
2	9	16	23	30
3	10	17	24	
4	11	18	25	
5	12	19	26	
6	13	20	27	
7	14	21	28	

NORTH SHORE, HAWAII: FROM NOVEMBER TO APRIL, BUT ESPECIALLY AROUND CHRISTMAS, THIS IS HOME TO SOME OF THE MOST FAMOUS SURF SPOTS IN THE WORLD. THIS PHOTO SHOWS WAIMEA BAY, WHERE THE BIGGEST WAVES ARE RIDDEN.

TUESDAY 23 SEPTEMBER
SURFING ROUND THE WORLD

I had such a good time on my camping trip that I've been bitten by the travel bug. So I've made up a map of places I want to surf before I'm old — before I'm 30, say. That sounds pretty old!

MUNDAKA IN NORTHERN SPAIN IS ONE OF THE LONGEST, MOST-POWERFUL LEFT-HANDERS (WAVE WHERE YOU TURN LEFT TO TRAVEL ALONG IT) IN THE WORLD.

ALSO...

California — Malibu, Blacks, the San Diego breaks, Mavericks... so many famous spots I can't fit them all in!

Indonesia — Bali, especially Uluwatu, and G-Land.

20

J-BAY IN SOUTH AFRICA IS ONE OF THE LONGEST, MOST-POWERFUL RIGHT-HANDERS. SHARKS ARE COMMON IN SOUTH AFRICA, AND EVERY YEAR SURFERS ARE ATTACKED. MIGHT LEAVE THIS TILL LATER!

NOOSA HEADS IN AUSTRALIA IS A POINT BREAK — WAVES BREAK ALONGSIDE A FINGER OF LAND POINTING OUT TO SEA. NEED ONE OF THESE ON THE LIST!

FISTRAL BEACH IN THE UK IS ONE OF THE COUNTRY'S TOP BEACH BREAKS. WHO SAYS THERE ARE NO GOOD WAVES IN BRITAIN?

NOVEMBER

3	10	17	24
4	11	18	25
5	12	19	26
6	13	20	27
7	14	21	28
1	8	15	22	29
2	9	16	23	30

Longboarding actually turned out to be a lot of fun. Catching the wave is way easier than on a board like mine, and so is keeping going on it. But the manoeuvres you do, especially cross-stepping, are really tricky. I kept trying nose rides and couldn't manage it. Maybe longboards aren't just for kooks after all...

SUNDAY 9 NOVEMBER
LOGGING IT

The water's colder now, and the winds have been on-shore gales for the last two weeks so no surfing. But today we had blue skies and no wind. The only trouble was, there were only tiny waves. I was so desperate to get in that Mark and I borrowed his dad's longboard and took it in turns to go out on it.

LONGBOARD LANGUAGE LESSON

• **CROSS-STEPPING** Walking up and down the board going sideways, by crossing one leg over the other.

• **HANGING FIVE** Standing so far forwards that you can get five toes over the nose of the board.

• **HANGING TEN** The trickiest longboard move — standing with all ten toes over the nose of the board.

• **KOOK** Someone who doesn't surf very well.

• **LOG** Another name for a longboard; also known as a Malibu board.

• **NOSE RIDE** Riding along on the wave standing on the very tip (the 'nose') of the board.

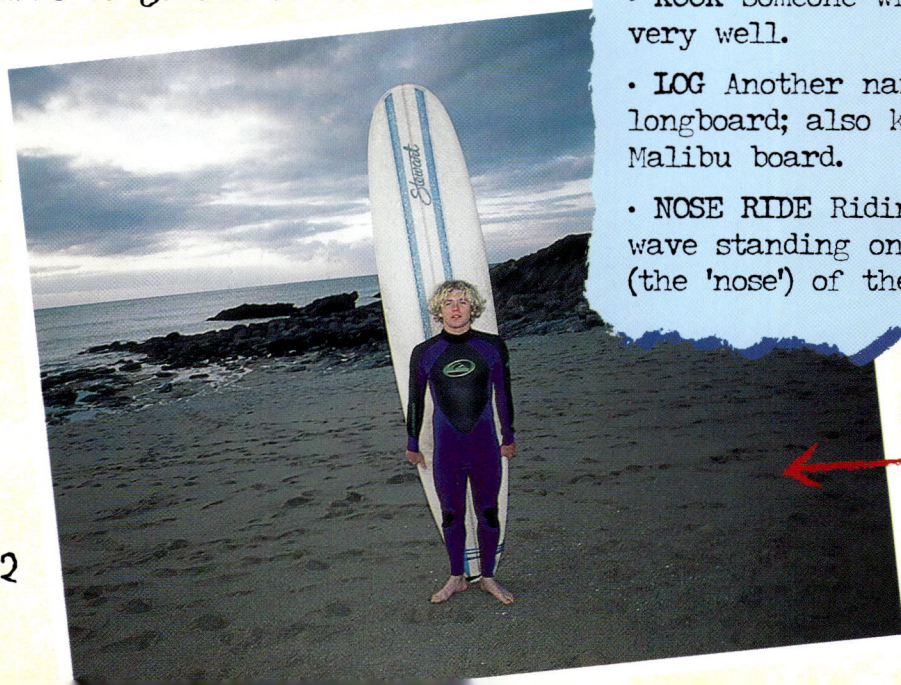

They really are long boards!

Joel Tudor, former World Longboard champion, about to get tubed.

Hanging five!

Nat Young, former World Surfing Champion, doing a drop-knee turn.

HISTORY

My longboard session the other day got me thinking about the history of surfing. Even before Columbus first reached America, people were surfing. In Hawaii the chiefs rode huge wooden boards called olos.

A Hawaiian surfer called Duke Kahanamoku was the main person who introduced surfing to mainland USA and Australia. It first became popular in the early twentieth century, and slowly spread around the world. In the 1960s surf movies first became popular, and surfing began to spread quickly. Now people surf almost everywhere there are waves!

Old pictures of surfers from the 1950s and 1960s.

DUKE KAHANAMOKU

Duke was a great surfer, but also the world's best swimmer. He won gold medals in the 1912 and 1920 Olympic Games. US President John F Kennedy even learned the 'Kahanamoku Kick' when he had swimming lessons!

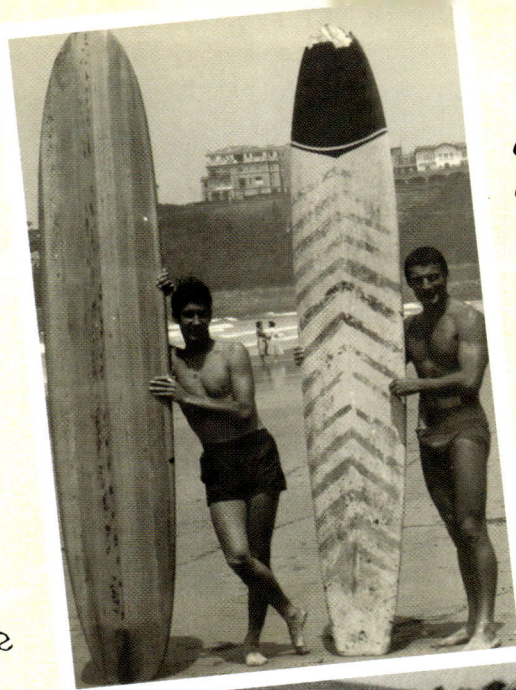

24

CLASSIC SURFING MOVIES

'Big Wednesday' – the story of three surfing friends in California in the 1960s and 1970s.

'The Endless Summer' – two surfers travel around the world searching for waves.

'Morning of the Earth' – Australian surfers at home and travelling to Bali in the 1970s.

MODERN SURF HEROES

Tom Curren (USA) – multiple world champion.

Tom Carroll (Australia) – Curren's great rival, also a world champion.

Mark Occhilupo (Australia) – the comeback king, who won the World Championship in 1999 after being out of the sport for years.

Tom Carroll: trademark top turn, Rocky Point, Hawaii.

Mark Occhilupo, at Pipeline, Hawaii.

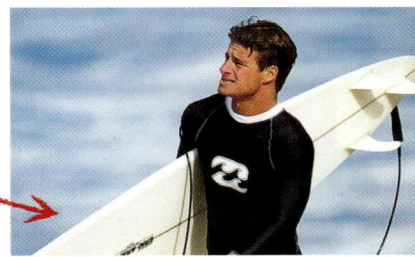

Tom Curren at a contest in Portugal.

25

NOVEMBER

3	10	17	24
4	11	18	25
5	12	19	26
6	13	20	27
7	14	21	28
1	8	15	22	29
2	9	16	23	30

SATURDAY 22 NOVEMBER COMPETITION

No surf, so no contest either. We decided to enter it about a month ago, but the contest's been cancelled because the sea's flat! Maybe next Saturday...

SATURDAY 29 NOVEMBER

Just finished my first surf contest! Had an excellent time, even though I didn't win. There were some great surfers there, but I still managed to get through to the quarterfinals.

We started with a briefing from the organizers. Each heat had three surfers in it, and at the end the best two went through to the next round. You're allowed to catch up to twelve waves in each heat, and the scores for your best four waves make up your final score. Each wave can get a maximum of 10 points, so in theory someone could score 40! I only managed 22 and 18 in my heats...

This guy made it to the final, but came second.

I rip! Really pleased with this cutback.

HOW WAVES ARE SCORED

The judges in a surfing competition look for:

1 The most radical manoeuvre.

2 Manoeuvres performed close to the breaking part of the wave.

3 The size and quality of the wave being ridden.

4 The length of the ride and number of manoeuvres performed.

The winner celebrates!

HEROES

Rain, rain and more rain. Also strong onshore winds that have ruined the surf. I feel like I've been trapped inside for weeks — probably because I have been! Have watched all my own videos, and all the ones I could borrow, about ten times each. There's only so much swimming in the pool and running to keep fit you can do!

All magazines have been read at least twenty times. Have decided to cut them up and paste my favourite surfers into the diary.

KELLY SLATER (from Florida, USA) won six world championships in the 1990s; doesn't really compete any more (doesn't need to: he must be a millionaire! I don't suppose he did it for the money, though...).

AERIALISTS Kalani Robb (from Hawaii) far left, Andy Irons (Hawaii) left and Shane Beschen (California) below. How do they go fast enough to get so high? These look more like skateboard moves than surfing ones!

ROCHELLE BALLARD from Hawaii. Other people say Layne Beachley is a better female surfer, but I like Rochelle because she takes off on huge waves even though she's really small.

29

SURF LANGUAGE

Aerial
A surfing move in which the board and rider leap into the air before coming back on to the wave and continuing to ride along it.

Beach break
A wave that breaks on a beach with either a sandy or stony bottom.

Bottom turn
The turn a surfer does at the bottom of the wave, setting themselves up for their next manoeuvre.

Break
Another word for a surf spot. Surfers talk about 'my local break', meaning the place where they go surfing most often.

Cutback
A move surfers make when they have got too far from the breaking part of the wave, which is the part that moves them along. The cutback is a turn that lets them change direction on the wave, to get back close to the breaking part.

Floater
A move where the surfer rides along a breaking, foamy section of the wave after it has broken.

Goofy foot
Someone who rides a surfboard with their right foot at the front of the board.

Heat
Part of a surf contest, where two, three or four surfers paddle out together and try to get the highest score for the waves they catch. The winner and, usually, the person in second get to go through to the next round.

Line-up
Where surfers sit on their boards waiting to catch a wave.

Malibu
Another word for a longboard, named after a famous surf spot in California on the beach at Malibu.

Onshore
Wind that is blowing from the sea on to the land. Strong onshores blow the waves flat or make them break badly so that they are impossible to ride well.

Out the back
At a point just behind where the waves are breaking.

Pitched
Thrown forwards out of control by the lip of a wave, resulting in being pummelled by the whitewater.

Diary of a SURF Freak

WITHDRAWN

Heinemann
LIBRARY

www.heinemann.co.uk/library

Visit our website to find out more information about **Heinemann Library** books.

To order:
☎ Phone 44 (0) 1865 888066
📄 Send a fax to 44 (0) 1865 314091
💻 Visit the Heinemann Bookshop at www.heinemann.co.uk/library to browse our catalogue and order online.

Produced by Monkey Puzzle Media Ltd
Gissing's Farm, Fressingfield, Suffolk IP21 5SH, UK

First published in Great Britain by Heinemann Library, Halley Court, Jordan Hill, Oxford OX2 8EJ, part of Harcourt Education.
Heinemann is a registered trademark of Harcourt Education Ltd.

First published in paperback in 2004
© Harcourt Education Ltd 2003
The moral right of the proprietor has been asserted.

Author: Paul Mason
Editorial: Catherine Burch
Series Designer: Tim Mayer
Book Designer: Vicky Short
Illustrator: Sam Lloyd
Production: Séverine Ribierre

Originated by Repro Multi-Warna
Printed in China by WKT Company Limited

ISBN 0 431 17533 0 (hardback)
07 06 05 04 03
10 9 8 7 6 5 4 3 2 1

ISBN 0 431 17538 1 (paperback)
08 07 06 05 04
10 9 8 7 6 5 4 3 2 1

British Library Cataloguing in Publication Data
Mason, Paul
Diary of a Surf Freak
797.3'2
A full catalogue record for this book is available from the British Library.

Acknowledgements
With thanks to *Carve* magazine for supplying all the photos. All photos by Mike Searle except the following: Chris Power **contents page top left** and **centre left**, pp. **13 top left, top right, centre left** and **bottom left**, 15 five photos on strip on right, **18** (all), **19**, **20 bottom**, **21 centre** and **bottom**, **25 bottom left**; Alex Williams front cover, **title page**, pp. **21 top, 23 right**; Nat Young Williams p. **23 bottom**; Yep/deRosnay p. **24 (all)**.

Every effort has been made to contact copyright holders of any material reproduced in this book. Any omissions will be rectified in subsequent printings if notice is given to the publishers.

Attention!

This book is about surfing, which is a dangerous sport. But this book is not an instruction manual or a substitute for proper lessons. Every year people die while surfing – make sure you aren't one of them. Get expert instruction, always wear the right safety equipment, and never go out on the ocean alone.